A Devotional Coming Out Of
My Own Life's Journey.

Thru The
Waters,
Thru the
Fire

WRITTEN AND ILLUSTRATED BY: THERESA ANDREWS

AuthorHouse™ LLC
1663 Liberty Drive
Bloomington, IN 47403
www.authorhouse.com
Phone: 1-800-839-8640

Published by AuthorHouse 02/14/2014

ISBN: 978-1-4918-2698-0 (sc)
ISBN: 978-1-4918-2697-3 (e)

Library of Congress Control Number: 2013919358

Unless otherwise noted, all Scripture quotations are taken from the New International

Version of the Bible.

Praise be to God and Father of our Lord Jesus Christ, the Father of compassion and the God of all comfort, who comforts us in all our troubles, so that we can comfort in any trouble with the comfort we ourselves receive from God.
2 Corinthians 1:3–4

Brothers and sisters, I do not consider myself yet to have taken hold of it. But one thing I do: Forgetting what is behind and straining toward what is ahead, I press on toward the goal to win the prize for which God has called me heavenward in Christ Jesus.
Philippians 3:13–14

DEDICATION

I give glory, honor, and praise to you, God, the Father, the Son, and the Holy Spirit. I dedicate this book to you, God, to use it as you see fit. You are my exceedingly great reward. Through the valleys, deserts, and storms of my life, you have matured me both organically and spiritually. I love you. Thank you, God, for loving me unconditionally.

I also dedicate this book to my mother and father, who have been consistently supportive of me during my struggles and celebrative of the good times in my life. They have never tired of caring and loving me. I can hear my father saying, "Be aggressive," and my mother, in her calming voice, saying, "I love you, Reese." They taught me that what matters most in life is my walk with Jesus Christ.

Alpha and omega,
Beginning and end.
Christ, my savior,
My deliverer and healer,
Everlasting Lord,
Father of my Lord, Jesus Christ.

God, who has a great plan for my life,
Holy Spirit, my comforter, counselor, and guide,
I give you the glory, honor, and praise.

TABLE OF CONTENTS

PREFACE

I wrote these poems while in tremendous emotional pain. I needed to express my innermost feelings of fear, hurt, doubt, and anxiety. It was a way for me to communicate not only my frustrations but also my gratitude to God. I asked the questions that we all ask when confronted with a life threatening disease. Why me? What do I do now?

In his book *The Problem of Pain*, C. S. Lewis wrote, "God whispers to us in our pleasures, speaks in our conscience, but shouts in our pain: it is His megaphone to rouse a deaf world."[1] I tried to be transparent with my poetry in order to help others. I found that, during my time of difficulty, the comfort from others who had experienced similar problems helped me most. I am encouraged, and I hope that you will be, as well, to move forward with your life in Christ. Please note that I do not pretend to be a theologian; I am currently a layperson in seminary, studying for the ministry.

---

[1] C. S. Lewis, *The Problem of Pain* (New York: HarperCollins Publishers, 2001), 91.

ACKNOWLEDGMENTS

I wish to thank the following:

The Holy Trinity: the Father, the Son (Jesus), and the Holy Spirit

My mother and father, Catherine and Jesse Cobb

My children, Jessica, Christopher, and Sabrina

My siblings and their spouses, Garry and his wife, Gwen; Marilyn and
her husband, Chris; and Michael and his wife, JoAnne

My deceased siblings, Tony, Brenda, and James

My dear friends who have been so supportive throughout my life and
new friends who have shared intimate times with me

In loving memory of Denise and many

Living in God's grace, Kofi

INTRODUCTION

God gave me the title of this book years ago. I had no idea what struggles I would endure before the book became a reality. God does not promise us that we, as Christians, will not have trouble. He does promise us that he will always be with us. A dear pastor introduced me to Isaiah 43:1–2, and I immersed myself in this passage while fighting cancer.

"But now, this is what the Lord says—he who created you, Jacob, he who formed you, Israel: Do not fear, for I have redeemed you; I have summoned you by name; you are mine. When you pass through the waters, I will be with you; and when you pass the rivers, they will not sweep over you. When you walk through the fire, you will not be burned; the flames will not set you ablaze."

Some of the other scriptures God used to help me during my most difficult times were 2 Corinthians 12 and Isaiah 41:10. "But he said to me, "My grace is sufficient for you, for my power is made perfect in weakness." In Isaiah 41:10 God says, "So do not fear for I am with you; do not be dismayed for I am you God. I will strengthen you and help you; I will uphold you with my righteous right hand." I read and prayed them over and over again until they became strong in my spirit.

After retirement, I was not sure what God wanted next for me. I told my sister Marilyn that what I did know was that God wanted me to write poetry about my battle with breast cancer. She said, "Then do it."

I have not written this book to give you a formula to follow. I have written it to let you know that God does bring us out of trouble. God does heal, and He is faithful. I am not better than anyone else. God is not a respecter of persons. Even now, I still have my problems. It has been said that we are either in a fight, coming out of a fight or going into a fight. The good news is that God goes through the water and through the fire with us. He delivered the three Hebrew boys, Shadrach, Meschach and Abenego in the fiery furnace, Daniel in the lion's den, Esther and Mordecai and the Jews from Haman, and Paul and Silas, who were locked in jail. My friend Linda always says, "If God delivered Daniel, why not deliver me?" Ask God, believe God, and let him do it his way.

I pray that this book will bless you and encourage your heart. I also pray that you will be able to say, "…we went through fire and through water, but you brought us to a place of abundance." (Psalm 66:12).

MY TESTIMONY

I was diagnosed with breast cancer in 2010. It was not easy to detect. The doctors took out a tumor in my right breast in September of 2010. They attempted a lumpectomy, but only four margins were cleared. I had three surgeries, two weeks apart. In October of that same year, I had a mastectomy and reconstructive surgery. My oncologist prescribed Tamoxifen for me. God healed me from breast cancer.

I did not have a lymph node problem; therefore, I was still able to draw and paint. God loves me, and I love him. He has given me a new appreciation for life. I have a renewed mind to serve God, and I am so grateful for his grace and mercy.

POEMS

CHANGE

Change is constant. During my struggle, I realized that I had to embrace change, not resist it. If I welcomed change, then I was able to see new possibilities and opportunities. It was difficult, but it was also attainable. I had to release God and myself from the mental box I had imprisoned us in. My mother, at age seventy-eight, said, "God is showing me things that I never saw before in his word."

Pray that God will open your eyes and ears to see and hear his heart.

Changed

Since this illness, life has not been the same.

God has called me by my name,

Set me worlds apart.

Gone are the guilt and shame,

All the heartache and blame;

His love he did impart.

No longer do I have to play the game.

He lovingly changed my heart.

That's why Jesus came.

Remember, he was God from the start.

He reminds us who he became—

Man in flesh, and yet fully God; beaten, broken, and lame.

But sin and death he overcame.

Amazing his creative work of art.

Now it is up to me do my part.

Philippians 3:14

John 1:1

Ezekiel 11:17–21; 36:24–28

Transformed

Oh, to be blessed,

Loved and caressed,

Calmed and distressed.

In the midst of the storm,

God comes to save me

And my mind to transform.

I hated the affliction and losing my norm.

Use it, Lord, me to conform,

Out of the uniform,

No more to perform.

I embrace this new, mature Christian form.

Romans 12:1, 2

Transition

I am in an unfamiliar place—

Never been,

Never seen,

Not even in between.

I humble myself, Lord, and seek your face

And ask for your grace

In faith

Putting one foot in front of the other,

Knowing my steps are ordered by my heavenly father,

I go in the strength of the Lord.

He and I are of one accord.

He is teaching me that patience

Is the essence

Of contentment this season.

Although I do not fully comprehend, he has his reason.

Psalm 71:16

Decision

I had so many mixed emotions, such a wide range.

Choosing contentment is an inside-outside change.

Now my priorities differently do I arrange.

Fear of boldness was the exchange.

I submitted to God, and my life he has started to rearrange.

Less concerned by the superficial.

No need for initials.

My mask shatters;

The make-up splatters;

My enemy scatters;

Transparency is what matters.

Thankful for numerous chances,

Bold and courageous advances,

Your grace that enhances—

My heart leaps and dances.

I made the decision to go forward,

Moving confidently onward.

My bright future I look toward.

No more gazing backward.

No longer confused, off-balance, veering sideward.

Not going wayward.

Gone is the coward.

Not in search of an earthly award,

But seeking a heavenly reward.

With all the blessings he has given me, I will be a good steward.

Knowing where my help comes from, I look upward—

Heavenward.

According to his call to help others stretch outward,

He continues to change my heart with his word.

Psalm 121:1

ADVERSITY

God never said I would not have trouble. He said that he would be with me when I went through the water and the fire and that he has overcome the world. The Holy Spirit resides in me, and I am able to do all things through Christ, who strengthens me. Indeed, as the scripture says, the Holy Spirit, the greater one, lives within me, and he is greater than he who is in the world (1 John 4:4).

God gives us resources, like people, friends, support groups, doctors, and nurses to help us through illnesses. I began to understand that I did not have to be miserable while going through my struggle. God was still on the throne—working behind the scenes—because I love him and am called to his purpose. "We have God's assurance that no matter how irrational the season turns out to be, no matter how long it takes or how painful it is for us to fully come to consciousness, God is with us (or in the Hebrew, Emmanuel)."[2]

Pray that God will uplift you and give you his perspective on your situation.

---

2   Renita J. Weems, *Showing Mary* (NewYork, New York: Warner Books, Inc. 2002) 21.

Simplicity

I have had to face adversity.
My friends and family remained alongside.
I hung on with tenacity;
I eliminated the pride.
I changed my identity,
Deciding in you to abide.

I weighed the complexity,
Letting go of things I held dear,
To find the simplicity
I knew you would provide
On the inside—
Knowing you love me.

John 15

Layers

I am sad,

Mad,

And glad.

God's love is so deep,

It makes me weep.

You see,

Miles away, just for me,

A word was spoken.

A wound is once again open.

I believed that I had forgiven,

And I thought I was healed.

But God has clearly revealed,

The hurt still in my heart.

So where do I start?

I have to turn the light on the hidden part

To get to the root and on the right track.

I have to peal the layers back.

Bad memories rush in like a flood,

But I remember why

Jesus shed his blood.

I begin to cry.

Yes, the pain is still tender,

But God is a fixer and a mender.

He has healed me before,

Now I need him even more.

I will yield and pray

And listen to what the Holy Spirit will say.

I do not intend

To give up or give in.

Yes, he is still working on me

To make me the person he desires me to be.

He will get the glory.

Through him, I will get the victory.

Psalm 34:18

Psalm 51:10

GRATITUDE

Most of my life was spent waiting for a situation or people to change or things to materialize or a goal to be realized. God taught me that it is important for me to be actively faithful and appreciative of what I already have during this waiting period. Plans are great, but I have to submit them to God, be willing to alter them when he asks me, and enjoy today. Life is a vapor—fleeting—and many precious moments can be lost if my eyes are riveted on the future. I remember my sister Brenda telling me to focus on what I have, not on what I don't have. I believe that what is for me is for me.

Pray that God will help you be grateful and thankful for each blessing in your life today and for what he did yesterday and will do tomorrow.

Thankfulness

Thank you.

Thank you, Lord, that I am cancer free.

Thank you for the mastectomy.

Thank you for the health of my body.

Thank you for your hand on me.

Thank you for my life and my dignity.

Thank you for managing the intricacy

Of medicine and natural healing, your grace and mercy.

Although I did not anticipate,

You helped me not to procrastinate.

It was not too late.

I realized that I was on trial, but

You helped me not to drown in denial.

The enemy I hate,

He tried to make me desolate

And isolate.

You gave me courage to let go

Of the image I had identified with so.

I had to be willing to lose to live,

To let go of pride, and my will to you I did give.

I cannot dwell on what people think,

Or into depression I will sink.

In a moment or a blink,

The stress will put my neck in a kink.

You help me to overcome.

Although the fight is not done,

The victory has already been won.

"…give thanks in all circumstances: for this is God's will for you in Christ Jesus."

1 Thessalonians 5:18

Gratefulness

I am grateful to be alive.

I long to remain steadfast in your peace.

Through the water, through the fire, I know what it means to survive.

During the raging storm—all fretting released—

And with your help, thrive.

I want all doubt and unbelief to cease,

To renew my drive,

To let go of anxiety and unrest,

And, at this new time and place, to arrive

And lay close to your chest.

Yes, I made it to the other side

To discover a newfound zest.

With your touch and love, my hope you revive.

I long for your word and intimacy with you at its best.

Isaiah 43:2

14

JOY

I was so frightened, confused, worried, and anxious that I lost my joy and could not sleep. Then I let go of control and of having to resolve everything myself, and in my way, I leaned on and rested in God. He restored my joy and my peace. He taught me also that rejoicing and choosing joy was a choice I could make no matter what my circumstances. Most importantly, he told me that he loved me unconditionally. Hearing that truth was priceless to me.

Pray that God will restore your joy and help you to see that your joy is in the Lord.

Rejoice

Oh, I make the choice
To lift my voice
And to rejoice.

For God has delivered me.
He has cleansed and set me free.

I will forever praise his name
Because I will never be the same.

Oh, I make the choice
To lift my voice
And to rejoice.

For God has been so good to me,
As Jesus died on Calvary.

I will forever praise his name
Because I will never be the same.

Oh, I make the choice
To lift my voice
And to rejoice.

For God has shown true love to me.
He made me part of his family.

I will forever praise his name
Because I will never be the same.

Philippians 4:4

"I will extol the Lord at all times;
his praise will always be on my lips."

Psalm 34

Restoration of Joy

Cancer has taught me that life is fragile.

Appreciate each day.

God showed me the way.

Singing again brought back my smile.

You see, it was gone for a little while;

Satan had taken it away,

Because he did lie, deceive, and beguile.

But in the meanwhile,

God taught me what to say.

He opened my eyes and restored my joy after a while.

Now I'm okay.

Each day I choose to rejoice and embrace my own style.

Yes, with God I intend to go the extra mile;

I know it will all be worthwhile.

Joel 2:25

Nehemiah 8:10

Psalm 51:12

Joy Is Not Chance

Joy is not chance,

Not happenstance.

It does not depend on my circumstance.

The joy of the Lord is my strength.

God wants my joy to be full—

To overflow—

And me to bask in the glow

Of being in his presence and walking in his will,

Knowing his promises he will fulfill.

It is a daily decision,

Yes, weeping my endurance of the night, but

Joy comes in the morning.

Rejoicing and singing,

No one can take my joy away from me.

It makes me glad,

Not sad,

When I put my trust in him.

Nehemiah 8:10

Isaiah 61:10

Enjoy

Chirping birds

Are what I heard

As I awoke

And God spoke

To my heart.

I created art

All around you,

For you,

For your joy,

And for you to enjoy

The budding of flowers in the spring.

See? I am doing a new thing.

I give you a new song to sing.

Isaiah 43:19

Negative Emotions

What a relief it was when I learned that I did not have to be controlled by negative emotions. They vary and are ever-changing. God showed me that I would lose opportunities if I let emotions such as fear, worry, anxiety, anger, resentment, and bitterness consume my life. They were choking me. Through the Holy Spirit, I could resist Satan and cut off negative thoughts at their inception. It was a mistake to be passive and just let negative thoughts overwhelm me. I could replace the negative thoughts with truths in the Bible, like

- God loves me unconditionally,
- I am the righteousness of God in Christ Jesus, and
- I can do all things through Christ who strengthens me.

Pride is an absolute killer. In fact, I can be prideful about so many things, even when I try to be humble. The Bible tells me that I can do nothing worthy apart from God. I believe Satan comes to kill, steal, and destroy, and many times he does it through pride. Eugene Peterson in *The Message Bible* says, "Get "Down on your knees before the Master; it's the only way you'll get on your feet" (James 4:10). Humility is the answer.

Pray that God will give you strength and power to pull down strongholds, interrupt wrong thoughts in your life, and replace them with Godly affirming thoughts. Lord, I purposely and intentionally humble myself before you.

Fear

A whole year

In the grip of fear,

Crying and flooded with tear after tear,

Wondering where you were,

If you were still near,

Satan whispering lies in my ear.

What are you going to do? He isn't your savior.

God is angry with you, and you have lost his favor.

Look at your doubtful behavior!

When would relief appear?

Then my praise changed the atmosphere.

I know you are here,

Making my cloudy thoughts clear.

I put on my armor and gear,

Ready to fight

Against principalities and powers of the air

Seeking to cause despair.

Not by power or might,

But by the Holy Spirit, I gain new insight.

"For the Spirit God gave us does not make us timid, but gives us power, love and self-discipline."

2 Timothy 1:7

Ephesians 6:10, 11,12

Pride

Pride.

It tries to make me hide

The pain that's inside.

It always seeks to divide.

Satan derides and misguides.

To humble myself is what I decide.

I remember that I need to be on God's side;

I cast my cares aside.

Then, Holy Spirit, you come alongside

To comfort and guide.

In you, I can always confide.

Negative emotions subside,

And under the shadow of your wings I abide,

Prompting me to let it show on the outside.

Oddly enough, then healing God will provide.

Proverbs 16:18

Worry

Worry can cause me to fall,
Does not move me forward at all,
Consumes time and mental space.
Peace it does replace—
Takes away sleep,
Makes me weep—
Keeps me from obedience
And causes impatience.
It's insidious,
Senseless,
Renders me useless,
Motionless,
Restless,
Speechless,
Makes problems seem endless,
And blocks my access
To success.
Worry irritates,
Aggravates,
Agitates,
Makes me hesitate,
Procrastinate.
Worry keeps me going in circles
While still expecting miracles.

Consumed and concerned about obstacles,

Makes me want to escape.

Over and over, playing the same tape.

It is destructive—

Never constructive.

In this, I do have control.

God watches over my soul.

He protects the birds of the air,

The grass of the field,

And me, if I yield

To him.

I cast my care,

No one can compare.

He is there,

Knows the number of my every hair,

My burden to share.

The battle is not mine, but his.

It is what it is.

Matthew 6

2 Chronicles 20:15

My Feelings

I can't rely on my feelings—

Up and down,

Down and up—

They will have me spinning.

Confused and dizzy,

Frustrated and uneasy,

In the trial,

Satan colored everything gray.

He left me speechless, no words to say.

I moaned,

Groaned,

Felt alone.

I screamed.

I cried,

"Life is just not fair!"

I was in despair.

The prince of the air—

What deception.

"Wait a minute!" I exclaimed,

"This is the day that the Lord has made."

I will rejoice and be glad in it.

Obey God in what he has already told me;

I have to face the truth about me.

It is a process.

God is working on me.

I need to change; to grow.

No condemnation, only conviction.

My feelings, I will not cede control.

Only Jesus can make me whole.

He is the restorer of the soul.

Psalm 23:3

Psalm 118:24

Galatians 5:22–25

GOD'S LOVE

The most liberating and life-altering truth is to know that God, almighty of all the universe, loves me unconditionally. What a treasure and a precious gem! Knowing that God loves me allows me to love and have patience with others, and it gives me courage and hope for tomorrow and security in today. Then, God tells me that nothing can ever separate me from his love; it makes me want to know him all the more.

Pray that God will help you to comprehend the depth, height, width, and breath of his love for you.

God Loves You

Holy Spirit, what a loving friend!

God hears my cry and offers

His helping hand to lend.

He is moved by my sigh.

My sorrowful heart he will mend.

I am the apple of his eye.

Only plans for my good does he intend.

His faithfulness I cannot deny.

Holy Spirit, his comfort he extends.

He bids me to draw nigh.

Despite all the needless worry I expend,

To worship him and exalt him high,

Gladly I submit my will and bend.

The flesh has to die.

To you, the all-wise God—alpha and omega, the beginning and the end.

John 14

Jeremiah 29:11

30

The Holy Spirit

As gentle as still waters,

Peaceful and quiet as it is after a storm.

As fluid as streams in wastelands,

There's a stirring, like raindrops causing rippling in ponds—

Anointing like rain showers,

Reviving like water on a dry plant,

Replenishing like rivers,

Floods, and overflows,

Spilling into the oceans of our spirits,

Nourishing like reservoirs of ground water—

As powerful as rushing waterfalls,

As satisfying as cool running water for our thirsty souls.

Psalm 23:1,2

You Have Value

You have value because God says so.
When Satan tells you are worthless, say no.
Your value is not in your possessions,
Not in your education, not in your professions,
Not in your children, your spouses,
Your cars, or houses.

When some are taken away,
God is still here to save the day,
And to show you the way.
God loves you because he chooses to.
His word is true.

Before you knew him, he knew you.
He loves you no matter what you do.
His love is unconditional,
Deliberate, and intentional.
Accept him as your Lord and savior and give him the glory due.

John 3:16
Ephesians 2
Psalm 139

God's Love

I never feel your absence,

For I am forever in your presence.

I am never alone,

Not on my own,

Sensing the wonder of your essence,

Or even if there is utter silence,

You made the promise that

You will never leave me.

I am immersed in your glory and excellence.

When life is so tough,

I offer up praise to you as a sweet incense.

When I feel like I've had enough

And the road is too rough,

In your word, you say to me,

"I love you. I have always loved you."

I reply, "I know it is true."

Hebrews 13:5

Romans 5:8

1 John 4:19

He Is There

He is there.
While I emotionally bleed,
He supplies my need.
His word I heed.
My soul he feeds.

I don't want platitudes;
I want to change my attitude.
Inside my mind, there is a feud.
Sometimes my thoughts are skewed.

How can I encourage them?
What can I do?
He responded, "Just be true.
Tell them how I mended you,
Made you anew."

I woke up from the nightmare
To realize he hadn't gone anywhere.
He was still there.
My life he did spare
Because he cares.

Philippians 4:19
Hebrews 13:5
Isaiah 26:3

Your Love

God, your love for me is higher than the highest mountain peak

And deeper than the deepest part of the ocean.

God, your love for me provides strength when I am weak

And heals my worst emotion.

God, your love for me is wider than the vastest breadth of the sky

And longer than the greatest dimensions of time and space.

God, your love for me wipes my tears when I cry

And comforts me in that sacred place.

Unfathomable—

The extent of your love.

Immeasurable—

My precious father above.

What shall separate me from the love of Christ, my king?

Absolutely nothing.

Ephesians 3: 16-19

Romans 8:35-39

GOD'S ATTRIBUTES

When I read the Bible, I learn more and more about God. I can rely and trust him because he does not change and he is everlasting and self-existing. I have great confidence in him. He is gracious and patient.

Sometimes I make mistakes. Other times, I am disobedient deliberately, but when I repent and confess my sin, he is faithful and just and forgiving.

Pray that God would give you greater understanding through his word.

Majesty

The majesty of God—
As I go for my walk,
With God, I talk.

The vast, cloudless blue sky provides the background for a beautiful scene.
The trees and grass are fully green.
Thank you, God, for all the beauty I have seen.

The waters in the pond are calm,
Like David describes in his psalm,
Acting as a healing balm.

All is peaceful and still,
Created by him to reveal
That the majesty of God is real.

Psalm 23

God as Deliverer

He is a deliverer in the midnight hour.
When all my life seems bitter and sour,
He is God and has all power.
I take refuge in him; he is my strong tower.
I do not have to run from Satan and cower,
For his bride, he has furnished a dower.
He cleansed me with his blood, like a rain shower,
Leaving me as beautiful and tender as a delicate flower.

Psalm 61:3
Psalm 91:2,3,14,15
Psalm 94:22

I Am God

I am God,

And there is no God besides me.

I am God;

I change not.

There is no shadow of turning with me.

I am God.

I will not lie.

You can trust me.

I am God.

I am able.

I can exceed anything you can

Ask or imagine.

Ask me.

I am God.

I am love.

I knew you before you were formed in

Your mother's womb.

I sent my son to die for you.

Embrace me.

I am God.

I do not break my promises.

I promise that I will never leave or forsake you,

Even into eternity.

You will always be with me.

I am God.

I am the bread of life.

Come and dine with me.

I am God.

I am the living water.

You will never thirst again with me.

I am God.

I am that I am.

With you, I make a better covenant—

I extend grace and mercy.

You will receive favor from me.

I am God.

I am the beginning and the end.

I am the self-existing one.

I am awesome,

And my purpose for you

Is not burdensome.

Cast your cares upon me.

I am God.

I am light.

You will not stay

In the darkness of night

If I abide in you

And you abide in me.

I am God.

I am your exceedingly

Great reward and shield.

Walk with me.

Talk with me.

I am God.

I am good.

I will not withhold anything good from you.

Every good and perfect gift

Comes from me.

James 1:17

Exodus

Isaiah 43

Genesis 15

Hebrews 13:5

1 Peter 5:7

Psalm 100

God as Healer

Yes, he heals.

It's real that God still does heal.

While Satan lies and tries to steal,

Kill, and destroy,

God fills, refills, and the anointing spills over,

Satisfying the thirsty soul, making the body whole.

He renews and restores the mind,

Mends the broken heart, cleansing every part.

Right before my eyes, God heals, and it comes as no surprise.

God is the same yesterday, today, and forevermore.

Let this be encouragement to you.

I'm a witness to his great goodness.

Gracious

You go near and far to be gracious.
You turn what was meant for bad to work out for good for me and for anyone
Who loves you and is called to your purpose.
You meet me where I am.
You are the God, "I am."

I am drenched with a torrential downpour of your blessings.
My heart overflows with the Holy Spirit's outpouring of grace.
You long for my embrace and for me to seek your face.

I expect good to happen to me.
I know that you alone can make me new,
Wash away my blues,
And show me endless love.
No one can match you, the one above
The one I love.

Isaiah 30:18

God's Promises

We can always count on God's promises;
What he said he will do, he will do.
He is never caught off-guard by surprises;
His word is forever true.

Another may see situations as relative compromises;
Our God is the same and never changes.
Sometimes his blessings have come in disguises.
He has been constant throughout the ages.

He wants you to be discerning and wise.
Let him fulfill his promises for you.
His calling, do not despise.
Do what he says to do.

If we study his word
Remember what we heard—
Be more like Christ; he has a divine plan for you.
Above all, God wants a relationship with you.
Draw close to God, and he will draw close to you.

Psalm 18:30

God's Greatness

Lord,

I'm praising you in the darkness.

You show yourself strong in my weakness.

Because of my past, I am a witness.

I am aware

Of your immeasurable goodness.

No one can compare

To your wonderful greatness.

How you care;

You lavish me with your loving kindness.

You clothe me with your righteousness.

You know my every hair.

You alone give me true happiness.

My burdens you bear.

Your amazing faithfulness—

You are always fair.

Your magnificent awesomeness—

You remove my blindness.

The love you share—

You turn my hopelessness into hopefulness.

Your light provides the brightness

And peaceful quietness

In moments of stillness.

In your presence, there is no more emptiness.

I find joy in fullness.

Embraced by your graciousness,

There is no end to your abundant mercy and tenderness.

Psalm 103:2–5

FUTURE

Quite frankly, at times, I was not sure I had a future. Satan had taunted me with thoughts of death and destruction. It was dark, ugly, and ungodly. I was passive and entertained these thoughts that created strongholds in my life. "Right action begins with right thinking. Don't be passive in your mind. Start today choosing right thoughts."[3] I sought help through therapy and a psychiatrist, which helped me enormously to see that I did not have to feel hopeless. Yes, my life was changing, but this change could be good if I allowed myself to see all the possibilities. My fears, doubts, worries, anxieties, and depression had become comfortable—and home to me. I stepped out into the water and, on faith, released those tormenting thoughts. I was determined, through God's help, to be optimistic about my future and to entrust it to him.

Pray that God will help you to see the possibilities in your future and to be excited about them.

---

3 Joyce Meyers, *Battlefield of the Mind* (New York, New York: Faith Words, 1995) 47.

Optimistic

My future,

Worrying about my future, wondering what's ahead,

My spirit tells me to trust and pray instead.

When I lay down on my bed,

All the lingering questions go through my head.

I have anxiety and try to calm myself with the scriptures I read.

I think of God and all the people he led by Moses, born of Jochebed.

I think of how he blessed Naomi and Ruth with Obed,

And of Jesse then with the man after his own heart, David.

I think of the five thousand that Jesus fed

With two fishes and five loaves of bread.

I think of how he healed the demoniac and into the pigs the demons fled.

I know and believe his wondrous works which he orchestrated, weaving each thread.

So why do I sometimes doubt what he said.

Can I be candid?

Being a Christian doesn't mean I never feel fear and dread,

But I will not let it consume me and to it be wed.

I thank God that he spared my life and that I am not dead.

I am looking forward to the days ahead.

Merciful, gracious, awesome God, the lifter of my head.

Psalm 3

Psalm 91

Matthew 6:33, 34

Starting All Over Again

I feel like I am starting all over again.

No, I don't say that to complain.

Please, let me explain.

God brought me through cancer, surgery, reconstructive surgery,

Depression, darkness, and back to life and light again.

Learning how to go forward after pain,

Looking back on some of my past with some disdain,

Mistaken about what accomplishments I did gain

And what possessions I was able to obtain,

Was I living in vain?

No, a greater glory from it all God will attain,

With him, a closer relationship I will maintain.

Safe under his wings, I will remain

From sin such as pride and lust, I intend to abstain.

And from the lust of the flesh and of the eyes, I refrain.

By grace and his spirit to sustain

And my joy to regain,

A fresh anointing I entertain,

I stand in his righteousness because he washed the crimson stain

Before the foundation of the world, his redeeming plan he did ordain.

His word in my heart I contain.

Psalm 91

1 John 2:16

This Moment

I know that I live in the moment today more than before,

Moments previously that I would ignore.

I am thankful for each new day more

Because God has spared my life; it is him I want to live for.

What a great God I worship and adore.

Psalm 90

PRAISE

I sincerely began to see depression and pessimism break when I started praising the Lord. Then I could expect good things and recognize that the glass was half full. God and I were intimate again in that special secret place.

Pray that God will empower you to praise and enter that inner place with him.

Praise

I praise you!

I praise you God

For the radiance of the sunlight

Keeping me through the dark of night,

For your love that brings me pure delight.

You let me accomplish not by power or by might,

But by your spirit, endurance, and insight

Because my future is bright.

You have promised to make my burden light.

Your embrace lifts me in the spirit to a greater height.

My God, who is all knowing, is always right.

Zechariah 4:6

Matthew 11:28

Praising You

Forever praising you
In spite of what I am going through.
Dancing in celebration of you
And all that you do.
Shouting hallelujahs, the highest praise,
My hands I raise
In awe of who you are,
The bright and morning star.
Singing songs of adoration
To you, my savior and creator,
My faithful intercessor.
Spreading the great proclamation,
Bowing down in humble exaltation,
To the Prince of Peace.
What sweet release!
Clapping, I make a joyful noise on one accord
To you, my Lord.
Basking in your presence,
Enjoying the fullness of your essence.
Before you, bringing
Myself as an offering
To you, King of kings.
You are Emmanuel, God,
With me.

Psalm 34:1

PROTECTION

I look back over my life and realize, when I thought I was in control, that God was protecting me in my naiveté. God allowed the cancer to be detected at the beginning stages. He gave me the courage and strength each year to go for my mammogram and to my gynecologist. The breast cancer I had was not easy to detect.

God worked in my life through prayer and through doctors. I did not have the miracle of divine healing. I had surgery to remove the cancer and a mastectomy. Often our society defines or identifies women based on our bodies. I realized that I was more than my breasts, and I would still be me if I no longer had them. God loves me, and I am valuable to him, my family, and my friends. I have changed my diet and my activity in an effort to be healthier. God has been my great reward and my shield.

Pray that God will keep you from harm and give you courage to do your part to sustain your life.

Early Detection

I am so grateful for early detection,

For your love and protection—

Despite others' rejections—

For my divine connection

To Jesus, the son who showed the Father's glorious reflection.

Where would I be without your love and affection?

Genesis 15:1

Romans 12:3

1 John 4

Stability

God gives me peace and tranquility.

He grants me my stability,

My security.

So what could be blocking it from being a reality for me?

Perhaps pride and vanity

While I go through difficulty.

I don't deny God's ability.

What I question is if he will do it for me.

Through this whole process, God has kept me from insanity.

You see, Jesus is my high priest, who has experienced my infirmity.

Although he still retained his deity, he took on humanity

And endured tragedy and calamity.

Now he seats at the right hand of the Father,

Making intercessions for you and me

In his priestly capacity.

No greater love has anyone than the Father, Son, and Holy Spirit,

My precious trinity.

Hebrews 4:14, 15

FAITH

In the many times I have quoted scripture, "faith is the substance of things hoped for, the evidence of things not seen" (Hebrews 11:1). Yet when I came to this time in my life, I needed faith to believe God loved me and that he had a good plan for me. My faith initially was strong, but when Satan, as he did with Job, brought multiple problems, I changed.

Then I staggered in my faith. I questioned God's love for me and had to build myself back up in the faith by reading, hearing, and meditating on his word. I had to dispel the myths and the lies that Satan had used to deceive me. In renewing my mind, God created a paradigm shift in my life, and I will never be the same.

Pray that the Lord will increase your faith to meet the challenges you are facing today and trust him with your tomorrow.

What is Faith?

Faith is . . .
Praising God in spite
Of everything not being right,
Singing when I cannot see light,
Lifting God up when fear urges me to take flight,
Calling out God's name when I sense loneliness in the night.

Faith is . . .
Giving God the glory in the middle of an awful situation,
Exalting God in the thick of the complication,
Worshipping God while fighting temptation,
Magnifying God during complex litigation,
Trusting God before the critical operation,
Giving thanks to God when you can find no justification,
Obeying God without immediate gratification.
Faith means belief in your own redemption.

Faith is . . .
Believing in God
And knowing that God rewards those who diligently seek God.
Without faith it is impossible to please God.
Through the obstacles I face, my faith is increased in God.

Hebrews 11:1, 6

Trust

In your presence, I am safe and secure,

Confident and sure.

I am learning to trust and believe and know

That you are on my side and with me everywhere I go.

You love me so.

You sent your only son to die for me long ago.

I am washed by Jesus's blood and made pure,

Able to be content and endure.

I will watch, pray, and be obedient in spite of my foe,

Encouraged as a Christian to mature and to grow,

To struggle against self-pity and woe,

To be content in whatever circumstances I undergo.

I praise you, the creator of all nature

And every living creature.

Proverbs 3:5, 6

RECURRENCE

Everyone who has had cancer deals with the issue of recurrence. I do not believe that God wants me to live my life in fear. He wants me to enjoy my life. Yes, I have to be real and make my appointments and go to them. But I choose to expect the best and believe I have complete deliverance and healing from cancer. However, if I have to go through the process again, I know God will go through it with me.

Pray that God will give you help to be responsible and enjoy your life as he has done for me.

Again?

If I am honest,

Yes, I think about recurrence.

I have some anxiety,

But I will not let it get the best of me.

When I have my medical visits,

The Holy Spirit

Gives me peace,

And the fretting ceases.

I have a calm assurance and belief

That I will not pass this way again,

And that gives me relief.

But If I do, God will still be on the throne.

I depend on him alone.

He has me in the palm of his hand.

I will obey his commands.

Nothing is a surprise to him,

And his plans for me are good.

Because I love him,

He works everything out for my good.

That is always understood.

Romans 8:28

FORGIVENESS

God showed me that there is no deliverance without forgiveness. In the Lord's Prayer, it says, "And forgive us our debts, as we have forgiven our debtors" (Matthew 6:12). Further in Matthew 6:14–15, it says, "For if you forgive other people when they sin against you, your heavenly Father will also forgive you. But if you do not forgive others their sins, your Father will not forgive your sins." It does not have to feel warm and fuzzy. I realize that forgiveness is not only forgiving others but also forgiving myself. "Grace isn't grace if we have to be good enough for it to apply to us."[4] I let go of all the guilt and shame to God so Satan could not torment me with it anymore. When the thoughts came, I resisted them like the fiery darts of the enemy. I had to be honest with myself and admit where there still was hurt, bitterness and resentment. Then, I asked God to cleanse me.

Pray that God forgives you for your sins and those who have sinned against you as well. This helps you to forgive yourself.

---

4   R.T.Kendall, *Revised and Updated Total Forgiveness* (Lake Mary, Florida: Charisma House 2007) 160.

Let go!

Forgive.

I need to continuously forgive,

To grow in Christ and live,

To earnestly love and genuinely give.

When I am wounded and bruised,

I can still be used.

If I forgive myself and others,

Care for my sisters and brothers,

I will not be a prisoner.

Pray for those who hurt me,

Whether intentionally or without a clue.

Try to relate,

Not isolate,

Or retaliate,

Or hate.

Release the pain

In order to have a greater gain.

A true Christian doesn't want to grieve the Holy Spirit,

So I let go and allow God to take care of it.

God won't be evil spirited.

As my stomach churns

Any guilt, I repent,

Any offense, I forgive,

And I learn that,

Through the release,

God heals and gives me peace.

I am stubborn and want control.

Through the struggle, God cleanses my soul.
Often, because of pride, I may not ask for forgiveness,
Showing my weakness.
God pries my fingers from what I am tightly holding onto.
Unforgiveness is an idol, too,
Consuming my focus and time anew.
God is jealous; he wants the praise he is due.

I learn from the mistakes in my past.
The hurt will not always last.
I can choose;
I will release and go forward, not stay stuck and lose.

Matthew 6

Mark 11:25

I Forgive Myself

I forgive myself completely.

Jesus forgives me fully.

He is plenteous in mercy.

I let go of guilt and shame,

Stop languishing and wallowing in blame.

Jesus knows my frame.

Jesus not only healed the broken hearted, the blind, and the lame.

He died on the cross and shed his blood for the same.

I call on his name.

To not forgive myself is saying that his blood was not enough,

When in fact, it was more than enough.

There is no condemnation.

Christ died on the cross, his redemption.

I confess my sin.

I let him cleanse me within.

His promise that he would be faithful and just

Cleanses me of all unrighteousness—

Because of his graciousness.

No, some say my sin is too great,

But God won't hesitate.

He won't leave me in that tormented state.

Satan will entrap, enslave, and snare me,

Use up my life with regret.

No, I don't need to fret.

God has good plans for me yet.

Ready, set, go!

Romans 8:1

Jeremiah 29:11

RELIEF

The storm is over now. I am still alive and well. I know that my God is a sustainer and a deliverer. He is the God of more than enough. God has taught me that when troubles come, I should run to him, not away from him. I should seek his face and dwell with him. Meanwhile, I still go for my medical check-ups and try to maintain a healthy diet and exercise regimen. All glory to God, the alpha and omega.

Pray that God will help you to endure and lean on and trust him always.

That sweet place

Oh, what relief!
Although Satan is a liar and a thief
And tries to keep me in pain and grief,
God, you listen to me
And answer me.
With you, I don't have
To be brief.
You are my God Almighty.
You give me authority
Over the enemy.
I believe; help my unbelief.
You know my every season as
Surely as you change the color
Of the leaves.
You want me to enjoy your creations, like
Crystal blue waters and the beautiful
Coral reef.
I worship you in that sweet place,
Surrounded by your amazing grace.

HOPE

Before I could reach faith, I had to find hope. There were times when I felt hopeless, but God sent me encouragement. I did not stay there. As long as I had God, I knew that I never had to be without hope. I did not have full deliverance, but I had hope that it would come. And it did.

Pray that God renews your mind so you are able to hope for better days.

Expecting good!

God, you tell me to wake up from my sleep.
Trying times have often caused me to weep.
Your tender mercies, I will keep.
I am full of hope.

I am expecting the good.
I know I will be able to cope.
My hope in you is deep—
Not superficial,
But substantial—
A strong confidence
In your omnipotence.

And even now you're working behind the scene.
You are my anchor, and on you I will lean.
Patient I will be
And let you teach me.

Psalm 25:4–5
Psalm 27:13, 14
Romans 4:18
Jeremiah 29:11

PRAYER

I believe in prayer. It is talking with God. I come to him in thankfulness and adoration of who he is. I confess my sins to him. God tells me to bring my requests to him. He invites me to pray for healing and that my needs are met for my family, friends, and country. Prayer changes me and gives me peace and assurance. David Ireland says and I agree, "Prayer is a gift from God."[5]

I know God answers prayer. It may not always be what I want—sometimes yes, other times no, and at other times, wait. I trust God and believe that he sees and knows what is best for me. Admittedly, it was difficult at times to pray during my struggle, but I did it out of obedience. The Bible says to pray always about everything and worry about nothing. I prayed and asked for the Holy Spirit's guidance in my decision making during the whole process.

Recently, I was talking to my daughter Jessica, and she put it so plainly. She said, "God, I trust you in this area of my life, but I need help in the other area." At times, I make God too small. He is able and willing to help me in every area of my life.

---

5   David D. Ireland, PhD., *The Kneeling Warrior* (Lake Mary, Florida: Charisma House, 2013) 48.

Pray that God will give you fellowship with him and a heart to pray.

Intimacy

At first it was hard to pray.
I did not know what to say,
But I cried out to you.
I asked for help.
You heard me;
You answered me.

I prayed out of obedience.
Praying calmed me,
Gave me assurance.
Others prayed for me, too.
Then I knew what to do.
I prayed for others.

You gave me what I needed and more.
You opened the door—
Intimacy to restore—
Even better than before.

Isaiah 30:19
Jeremiah 29:12
Psalm 34:17
James 5:16
Revelation 5:8

DELIVERANCE

God does deliver. I am a living witness that he has taken me through the water and the fire to the other side. I believe there is a natural and spiritual side to life. God does his part and expects me to do mine. Christianity is not a passive faith.

God asked the man, "Do you want to get well?"(John 5:6). I had to want to be healed and to seek and avail myself of resources. I had to humble myself and accept care and help from friends and family. In the past, I was wrong to be overly independent and isolate myself. The truth is I need people and people need me. We need each other in the body of Christ.

Pray that God will send you encouragement to do your part in your recovery.

Pulled Out!

God, you reached down and pulled me out

Of the muck and mire,

Where I was stuck,

Out of the slippery quicksand

To help me boldly stand.

I lifted up my hands.

Many rejected me.

I was deceived plenty,

But you reminded me

That the Holy Spirit resides in me.

I bow the knee.

I am excited about the future possibilities.

I am your beloved.

I completely savor

The knowledge that I have your favor.

You say so in your word,

Which I have frequently heard.

I die to self,

Exalt you above myself,

Put my ego on the shelf.

My purpose is to glorify, magnify, praise, and worship you.

My hope is in you.

Thank you for your mercy and power.

In this same hour,
I want to be quick to obey,
Quick to do what you say.

Thank you for your goodness
And deliverance.
I serve you with gladness.
Help me to be your witness.
You are the one I bless.
I will flourish and grow
And be faithful to do what I already know.

GOSPEL MUSIC

Gospel music has been an integral part of my Christian experience. It has been an encouragement for me during some of the darkest times of my life. God uses gospel music to help me maintain my joy and cast my care toward him. The Holy Spirit used it to minister to me while I was going through my fight against breast cancer.

Pray that God will bless you with music that comforts and encourages your soul.

Sacred Music

Gospel music gave me hope when I felt hopeless,

Restored my emotion when I was emotionless.

Times when I could only groan

And moan,

It encouraged my worn and tired soul.

It mended broken pieces and made me whole.

It gave me strength to go on,

Courage to hold on.

This sacred music gave me the inspiration,

Cause for celebration,

And great jubilation.

It lifted my spirits

When my heart needed to hear it.

The Holy Spirit

Invited me into the inner courts.

It was genuine and brought me to that place of intimacy with Jesus,

For a moment releasing the burdens and cares,

So I could truly praise and be in the Lord's presence,

Offering up my story.

My thanksgiving was sweet incense

Surrounded by his glory.

It broke the stronghold,

Provided peace untold

And joy manifold,

And I saw his good plan for me unfold.

Yes, I could overcome

And, with God's help, become

The woman he called me to be—

Truly, truly set free—

And on my way to recovery

And everlasting victory.

Thank you, my ancestors, grandparents,

And parents,

For this oral tradition and precious gift

You have given me in gospel music.

RESTORATION

I rejoice in God because he is a God of restoration. Jesus restored my sleep, joy, peace, hope, faith, strength, dreams, self-confidence, health, right mind, and intimacy with him. I could hear the voice of the Holy Spirit guiding me again. Jesus not only restored me to health, but also he gave me a new zest for life, a new attitude, a new dance, and a new song. What I gained in this struggle was far more than what I lost.

I am expecting great things ahead. God does exceedingly—abundantly—more than I could imagine or even expect. His love for me is so great that I still cannot fully comprehend the depth, height, width, and breadth of it.

Pray for restoration of what God gave you and the ability and desire to let go of the past.

Ideas, dreams and visions

I looked up, and there it was—
Restoration.
Like David at Ziglag or Job
Weeping through the night,
Now it was morning.
I was singing,
Praising,
And dancing.
My sleep and peace were respite once more.
A bright smile replaced the frown I wore.
The God, whom I adore,
My joy and right mind, he did restore
And placed before me an open door.
Opportunity like I never knew before—
Fresh ideas, dreams, and visions galore—
My desire is to dwell with him forevermore.
I could see and hear the Holy Spirit again,
Have the right perspective on sin,
I could begin again.

I shed the old worn clothes and put on the new,
All the time in awe of what God can, did, and will do.

1 Samuel 30
Job 42:10, 12
Psalm 23:3
Psalm 30:5
Psalm 66:23

THE WORD OF GOD

I consistently and constantly relied on the word of God during my battle. I read it over and over. I meditated on it. I sought answers to my questions concerning sickness and healing. I longed for a closer walk with the Lord. Reading the Bible provided encouragement and knowledge that God loved me unconditionally and helped me understand God more.

Pray for discipline to read and study God's word, no matter your circumstances.

Your Word

Lord, your word,

I heard.

I am ready for war; it is a sword.

On it, I meditate;

I focus and concentrate.

I pray, Holy Spirit, that you will illuminate

My understanding

Of Satan—the word I did reiterate.

Lord, I hide it in my heart that I might not sin against you.

Your word is alive and true

When the only way out is through.

May I not only hear, but also do.

Sometimes the Bible gives me clear direction

And precise instruction.

Other times, it gives principles for action,

For response and reaction.

The grass and the flowers will die.

But the word of God does not lie or die.

It shall stand forever,

Come whatever.

I need your word to live.

Jesus, you are the living word of God.

Psalm 1:2

Psalm 119:11

Joshua 1:8

Isaiah 40:8

Isaiah 55:11

John 1:1

Ephesians 6:17

Romans 10:17

Hebrews 4:12

PRAYER FOR SALVATION

If you have not accepted Jesus as your Lord and savior, you can do it right now.

I Humble Myself

God, you said, "Offer yourself
As a living sacrifice.
Put your ego on the shelf.
Be willing to pay the price.
Deny the self
And follow me."

With you at the helm,
I do not have to be overwhelmed.
Your direction is clear and simple—
"Be my disciple
And follow me."

Pray to God, and say, "I confess with my mouth, and I believe in my heart that Jesus died on the cross for my sins and rose from the dead and now sits at the right hand of the Father, making intercession for me. I accept Jesus as my Lord and savior, and I repent of my sins."

God bless you and welcome into the family of God.

A Prayer

My prayer for you is that
God grants you
Wisdom and understanding,
The ability to make good choices about the spiritual and the natural,
Knowledge of his love for you,
And blessings for you and your family.

Printed in the United States
By Bookmasters